Gus Finds God

MW00891451

Written by Michael P. Foley

Illustrated and Designed by Andrea Dahm

EMMAUS ROAD PUBLISHING

STEUBENVILLE, OHIO
www.EmmausRoad.org

EMMAUS ROAD PUBLISHING
1468 Parkview Circle
Steubenville, Ohio 43952

Text © 2018 Michael Foley
Design and Illustrations © 2018 Andrea Dahm
All rights reserved. Published 2018
Printed in the United States of America

Library of Congress Control Number: 2018938918
ISBN 978-1-947792-60-9 hardcover / 978-1-947792-61-6 paperback /
978-1-947792-62-3 ebook

Quotations from book ten of the *Confessions* are taken with permission of the publisher from *The Confessions of Saint Augustine*, 2nd ed., trans. F.J. Sheed, ed. Michael P. Foley (Indianapolis, IN: Hackett, 2006). All rights reserved

Cover design and layout by Andrea Dahm

Darling Kinley

March 28th 2019
Divine Mercy Sunday.

Congratulations on your
First Holy Communion!
I love You.
Dad.

We lovingly dedicate this book to
our own "gifts from God"

To Mike's children: Catherine, Mary, James,
Peter, Monica, and John

To Andrea's children: Beatrice and Esther

To Mike's wife Alexandra,
whose inspired idea this book was

To Andrea's husband Brandon

Finally, in memory of Mike's mom, Lucille Monica,
the first to read him children's books

And in memory of Andrea's mom, Paula, who always
encouraged her in her pursuit of art and design

Introduction for Mom and Dad

The little book you hold in your hands is inspired by book ten of St. Augustine's *Confessions*. In fact, most of the lines are taken word-for-word from Frank Sheed's translation of this immortal Christian classic.

St. Augustine of Hippo (354-430) was the greatest Christian thinker of the first millennium. A notorious sinner turned saintly bishop, he wrote about his conversion to Christ in his *Confessions* when he was forty-three. For a long time the *Confessions* was the second-most-read book in all of Christendom, second only to the Bible itself. No other non-biblical writer has influenced Christianity as much as Augustine.

One of Augustine's greatest hurdles in converting was understanding how God is really real but not how a physical object like a star or tree is real. And one of his goals in writing the *Confessions* was to help others overcome this hurdle as well. In addition to the Holy Bible, Augustine turned to two other "books" written by God that help explain who and what God is.

The first is the "Book of Nature." Augustine took seriously the Psalm verse, "Let the heavens and the earth praise Him: the sea, and every thing that creepeth therein" (68:35 [69:34]). Here is what he says about that Psalm:

> Some people, in order to find God, read a book. And there is a certain great book: the very appearance of created things. Look above you and below you! Pay attention to it! Read it! So that you could get to know Him, God did not write letters in ink, but before your very eyes He placed the things He had made. What louder voice can you ask for? Heaven and earth cry out to you: "God made me!"

But as amazing as the Book of Nature is, the second book is even more amazing—the mysterious "book" of our own minds. The very fact that we can remember and know things is evidence that we are made in the image and likeness of God and that God makes it possible for us to be enlightened by knowledge, for He is "the true light which enlighteneth every man that cometh into this world" (Jn 1:19). How could a mere creature know things that are eternally true unless he is somehow being illuminated from Above?

Gus Finds God starts with the Book of Nature and then moves to the Book of the Mind; using Augustine's quaint and easy language, the story fires a child's imagination and introduces him or her to a whole new way of viewing the world around and within. That doesn't mean, of course, that children will understand the deep truths about God and the mind right away: after all, even mighty philosophers and scientists sometimes come up short in this regard. But it is our hope that *Gus Finds God* will plant seeds in the hearts of its readers young and old, seeds that will help them grow in self-knowledge and in the knowledge and love of God. It is our hope that *Gus Finds God* will create a thirst so very neatly expressed in one of Augustine's prayers: "O Lord, may I know You, may I know myself!"

Lastly, in an effort to water these seeds further, we include "Some Questions to Talk About" at the back of the book. You will be amazed by how your children react to this book and by the questions they ask. Even if you can't answer them perfectly, the important thing is that they are growing in wonder about our loving Creator.

— Mike Foley and Andrea Dahm
FEAST OF ST. AUGUSTINE
August 28, 2017

Once upon a time there was a little boy named Gus.

One day Gus and his mom were talking.
"WHO IS GOD?" Gus asked.

"Well," his mom replied, "God is our Father who made us!
He is all-powerful, all-knowing, and He loves us very much."

"Wow!" Gus said. He was impressed. "When can I see him?"

"Oh no," his mother laughed.

"God can't be seen
with the eyes,

He can't be heard with the ears,

He can't be smelled
with the nose,

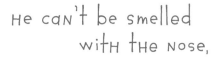

He can't be tasted
with the mouth,

and he can't be
touched with
the hands.

GOD IS
INVISIBLE."

3

"In—vis—i—ble?" Gus repeated.

This made Gus very confused,
    so he decided to look for God himself.

Gus went outside and looked at the land around him.

"Mr. Land," he asked,

"ARE YOU GOD?"

"No," moaned the land in a dry voice, "I am not."

ZOO

So Gus turned to all the things that
live on the land, all the tame animals
and all the wild beasts
and all the creeping things that
crawl upon the earth.

"ARE YOU GOD?"

"No," they all replied, making the same confession.
"We are not he."

Next Gus went to the deep sea and all
the wondrous creatures in it.

"Mrs. Sea," he asked,

"ARE YOU GOD?"

"No," splashed the deep sea
and all the creatures in it,

"We are not your God.
Seek higher."

So Gus looked up and said to the winds that blow.

"Mr. Wind," he cried,

"ARE YOU GOD?"

"NO," howled the wind and all
the creatures of the air with it.
"We are not God."

OBSERVATORY

8

Then Gus went even higher,
and looked way up to the sun,
the moon, and the stars.

"Excuse me," he called out to
the fiery lights in the sky,

"are any of YOU GOD?"

But they all said back to him,
"Neither are we God whom you seek."

9

And Gus said to all the
things he could see:

"Tell me something about God,
since you are not he.
Tell me something about him.

"And they all cried out in one great voice:

"HE MADE US!"

Gus went back inside. He was sad that he
had not found God, and he was still very confused.

So Gus began to think some more.
"If God is not any of the things around me,"
he said to himself,

"maybe he is
something IN me."

Gus looked and looked, but he could not find God inside him.

"Well," Gus asked, "if God is not in my body, where could he be?"

Gus thought very hard, and then he remembered something that his mom had once said. She had told him that there was more to him than just his body, that he had a soul which would live forever and ever.

"My soul must be very special,"
    Gus thought. "Don't all those animals
I questioned have the same senses that I do?

Can't an eagle see?

Can't a hound dog smell?

Can't an elephant hear?

In fact, they can do these things better
than I can! But there is something
I can do that they can't: I can question
the things I see, smell, and hear."

13

So Gus turned to
the power of his soul,
and there he found his memory.

And oh was he amazed!

14

Gus saw that his memory was like
a vast palace with many, many rooms.
And each of these rooms contained
many, many memories.

Gus Realized that He could Remember
all kinds of things.

He could Remember
what his Home looked like,

and He could Remember
what a guitar sounded like,

and He could Remember
what flowers smelled like,

and He could Remember
what a chocolate chip cookie
tasted like,

and He could Remember
what His shaggy dog felt like.

Sometimes, when Gus tried to remember something,
a great crowd of memories would jump out and ask,
"May it not be we that you want?"
Gus would have to brush them away
with the hand of his mind and say, "No."

At other times, the memory would come up in a nice,
proper order. This is what happened anytime
Gus said something by heart.

Our Father... Who Art in heaven...
...Hallowed be Thy name...

Sometimes, it was easy to remember something.

At other times, it was very hard
to remember something.

But Gus wanted to go farther into His soul,
and so He came to a second kind of memory.
This other kind of memory was not like the physical
things Gus could remember; it was a memory
of things that are always true. Gus could remember,
for example, that one plus one is two, and He knew that
a whole circle is bigger than part of a circle.
These are things that are always true
and always will be true.

SENSES

Gus wanted to know how
these truths had ever gotten
into his memory in the first place. So he
ran his mind over all the doorways of his body,
his senses, but he could not find any door
by which they could have come in.

Gus's eyes said to him,
   "If these truths had any color,
   we reported them to you."

And his ears said to him,
   "If they made a noise,
   we gave you notice of them."

And his nose said to him,
   "If they had any smell, they
            went in through us."

And his taste buds said to him,
   "Unless there was any taste
         in them, there is no use
         in our being asked."

And his sense of touch said to him,
   "If the thing is not a body,
         I did not handle it,
         and if I did not
            handle it, I did not
      report it to you."

21

So Gus realized that these truths
were ALREADY in his memory,
even though he may have needed a teacher
to help him find them there and
even though he needed words or pictures
to help him remember what they were.

But Gus wanted to go even farther into his soul,
so he came to a third kind of memory,
the memory of all his feelings.

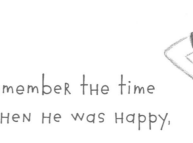

Gus could remember the time
last summer when he was happy,

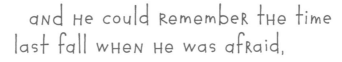

and he could remember the time
last spring when he was sad,

and he could remember the time
last fall when he was afraid,

and he could remember the time
last winter when he really,
really wanted to have a new toy.

23

In fact, Gus could remember all these old feelings
even when he wasn't feeling them now.
Gus could remember being happy when he wasn't happy now,
and he could remember being sad when he wasn't sad now.
Gus could even "picture" these feelings,
even though it is hard to picture something like a feeling.

Gus saw that his memory was vast and wonderful. Inside it were all things he could remember seeing and hearing and smelling and tasting and touching. Inside it were all the things he knew to be true. And inside it were all the feelings of joy, sorrow, fear, and desire that he could remember feeling. What a great thing memory is! How many nooks and crannies it has, filled with so many things!

Without our memory, where would we be?

But is God
IN Gus's memory?

God is not something he can remember like his mom.
God is not something he can remember like an addition table.
God is not something he can remember like
his happy or sad times.

But God has to be somewhere in Gus's memory.
How else could Gus recognize God's name every time he heard it?

Suddenly, the answer came to him.

God, Gus realized, was not only
in his memory in a very special way,
but God was above his memory.

God is like a very bright light that lets us
see all our memories. God is higher than
our souls, and He is higher than
anything we can see or hear or smell
or taste or touch. But this doesn't mean
that God is far away from us.

Oh no, God is so close to us that
He is even closer to us
than we are to ourselves!

"Mom was right," Gus said.

"God isn't someone I can see,
but that doesn't mean
He's not real. Not at all:

He's more real than I am,
and He makes
everything else real!"

And so Gus ran to his mom and told her
all the things he had learned about God.
Gus's mom was so excited that they both
knelt down to thank and praise God.
Gus's mom then led them in a prayer
she had read and prayed many times:

"Late have I loved thee,
oh beauty, ever ancient, ever new:
late have I loved thee!
For behold, you called to me
and broke upon my deafness.
You sent forth your beams
and shone upon me
and chased away my blindness.
You breathed your fragrance upon me,
and I drew breath
and now pant for you.
I tasted you, and now hunger
and thirst for you.
I touched you, and I have
burned for your peace."

Gus went outside. He went on with his day, thinking how great God is.
And Gus was filled with joy.

the end

Some Questions to Talk About

Note: These discussion points aren't necessarily intended for you to read verbatim to your child, but for you to put into your own words—or at least to prepare you for their questions!

If I can't see God, as Gus and his mom say, then what about Jesus? Isn't He God? And aren't there pictures of Him, like Bible illustrations, icons, and crucifixes?

Yes, Jesus is fully God, and He is also fully human just like us, but it is only His humanity that we can see. No one can see Jesus' divinity with their bare eyes, which is why many people, like the Pharisees and Pontius Pilate, did not recognize that Jesus was God. That is why it is important to have faith (by grace of the Holy Spirit), which helps our soul "see" Jesus' divinity.

Does creation really "speak"?

Well, yes and no. Mountains and rivers and all creatures great and small don't use words like we do, but their very existence tells us that they are beautiful things that are part of a big, beautiful world that did not create itself. In this sense, creation "speaks" of the fact that it was made by a good and loving God.

When Gus goes around asking questions about all the things he can see, he starts with the land and all land creatures; second, he goes to the sea and all sea creatures; third, he questions the wind and all creatures of the air (birds, bats, bees, and flying insects); and fourth, he turns to all the "fiery" heavenly bodies in outer space. Why this order?

Gus's search follows the ancient idea of the "four elements" of the world. Before the discovery of atoms and molecules, four things—earth, water, air, and fire—were considered the basic building blocks of everything else. They can still be a pretty fun way to think about things.

After speaking to all creation, Gus turns to his memory. Is our memory the same thing as our soul? Is it immortal?

Our memory is not the same thing as our soul. Our soul is what gives life to our body, and our memory is a very important part of our soul. In fact, there is a way in which we would not be ourselves without our memory, for it is our memories that help to make us who we are. And while not every memory of ours may be eternal, the power of memory is indeed an immortal part of our immortal soul. Without it, we'd forget to praise God in Heaven!

Gus discovers three kinds of memories: a memory of physical things, a memory of truths, and a memory of feelings. What's up with that?

Well it's true, isn't it? A memory of physical objects or of people is a different kind of memory from a memory of, say, math or logic; and these two kinds of memories are different from a memory of your past emotions. And God, in turn, is different from all three kinds of memory. For instance, God is not just one truth (like 1+1=2) but He is the Truth (see Jn 14:6). And yes, God is Love (see 1 Jn 4:8), but that doesn't mean God is one of my emotions.

Your three kinds of memory, by the way, also line up with the three kinds of things you can ever desire. You can desire: 1) physical things or physical pleasure, like money or food or a good massage); 2) knowledge or wisdom, like knowing how a car or computer works; or 3) emotional satisfaction, like winning a game or being praised by someone you respect. Pretty much every human longing fits into one of these three categories.

Creation keeps telling Gus to "seek higher," and Gus eventually finds God "above" his memory. So, where is God? Is He above the stars? In me? Above me?

Well, all of the these and more. God is everywhere because all His creation is present to Him, but He is also above creation (including our minds) in the sense that He is the mighty Creator and we are His lowly creatures. The really hard part in all this is realizing that God is not in space; space is in God. Chew on that one!

This, incidentally, is partly what people mean when they speak of God as Transcendent Being. God is unlike anything else; He transcends or goes beyond all His Creation (from lowly bugs to lofty angels), and He is even uniquely different from uncreated or eternal truths.

So, what does it mean when it says that God is like a very bright light that lets us see all our memories?

God is not a part of our minds, but He makes it possible for our minds to remember and know things. Think of it this way: when you get an insight into something, when "the light goes on in your head" and you suddenly grasp the solution to a problem or a riddle, doesn't it feel like that insight is a gift, that it hits you from the outside? One way to think of the little light that goes on in your head when you have an insight is that it is participating or "tapped into" the Light "that enlighteneth every man that cometh into this world" (Jn 1:19).

I'm wondering about the Eucharist or Holy Communion. Since Jesus says "This is My body" and "This is My blood" (Mt 26:26-28), aren't I seeing and tasting the Son of God when I receive Holy Communion?

The Eucharist is the Body and Blood of Jesus Christ, but our senses can't know that. All they can taste or see is what appears to them to be bread and wine. Only our soul, through faith, can know that it is Jesus's risen and glorified Body that we receive in the "breaking of the bread" (Lk 24:35).

How come the prayer at the end mentions God being touched, tasted, etc? Based on everything else in the book, isn't that impossible?

It is impossible physically, but in this prayer Gus and his mom are really talking about their souls "touching" and "tasting" God, not their hands or tongues. They can talk this way without getting confused because they now know the difference between what their souls can sense and what their bodies can sense. God is not a physical thing, but every physical thing has God's "fingerprints" on it. Because of that, the world around us somehow gives us a glimpse of God. Here is a quote by St. Augustine that explains what he is getting at:

> But what is it that I love when I love You, O God? Not the beauty of any bodily thing, nor the order of seasons, not the brightness of light that rejoices the eye, nor the sweet melodies of all songs, nor the sweet fragrance of flowers and ointments and spices: not manna nor honey, not the limbs that carnal love embraces. None of these things do I love in loving my God. Yet in a sense I do love light and melody and fragrance and food and embrace when I love my God—the light and the voice and the fragrance and the food and embrace in the soul, when that light shines upon my soul which no place can contain, that voice sounds which no time can take from me, I breathe that fragrance which no wind scatters, I eat the food which is not lessened by eating, and I lie in the embrace which satiety never comes to sunder. This it is that I love, when I love my God (*Conf* 10.6.8).

CPSIA information can be obtained
at www.ICGtesting.com
Printed in the USA
BVHW021017210419
545809BV00037B/87/P

9 781947 792616